T0034020

A SUPPLEMENT TO
A MODERN APPROACH
TO CLASSICAL GUITAR

ARRANGED, EDITED, AND PERFORMED
BY CHARLES DUNCAN

To access audio visit:
www.halleonard.com/mylibrary

Enter Code
5089-3871-9330-7327

Cover guitars courtesy of Cascio Music Co.

ISBN 978-0-7935-1795-4

7777 W. BLUEMOUND RD. P.O. BOX 13819 MILWAUKEE, WI 53213

Visit Hal Leonard Online at
www.halleonard.com

PREFACE

This book contains 32 classical guitar duet arrangements for either recreational or instructional use. The sequence of pieces is based on the difficulty of the first guitar part. However, the level of difficulty is indicated at the beginning of each piece for both parts. The general criteria for grade levels are:

Level	Criteria
1	Single notes on treble strings in simple rhythms.
1A	Single notes throughout first position.
2	Notes played together, simple arpeggios in first position, single notes to third position.
2A	More elaborate rhythms, occasional small barre chords, slurs, single notes to fifth position.
3	General intermediate-level playing skills.

The accompanying play-along audio will allow you to practice and play each piece as a duet. Both parts are recorded, with the first guitar on the right channel, and the second guitar on the left channel. Use your left-right balance control to tune out either channel while you play the other part yourself.

The tempo is indicated at the beginning of each piece by two measures of metronome clicks. A tuning track is also provided.

TABLE OF CONTENTS

MINUET

Johann Krieger
(1651 - 1735)

ALLEGRETTO

Fernando Sor
(1778 - 1839)

ALLEGRO

Wolfgang Amadeus Mozart
(1756 - 1791)

ENTRÉE

Leopold Mozart
(1719 - 1787)

ANDANTINO

Mauro Giuliani
(1781 - 1839)

9

ANDANTE

Fernando Sor
(1778 - 1839)

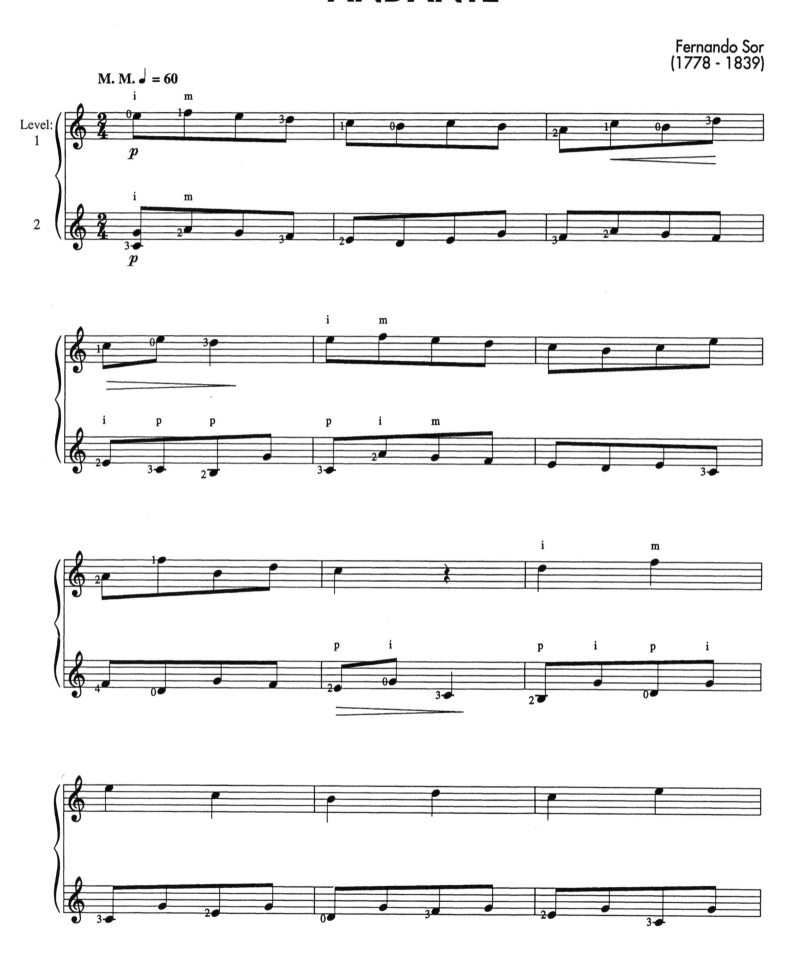

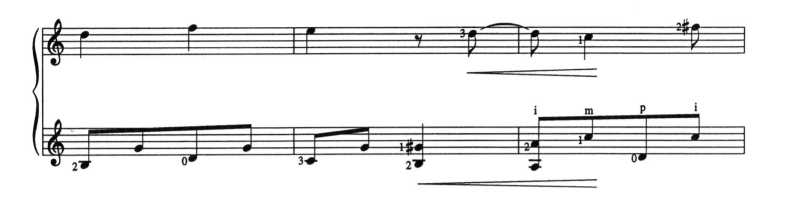

ODE TO JOY

Ludwig van Beethoven
(1770 - 1827)

WHAT THEN IS LOVE

Philip Rosseter
(1575 - 1623)

PRESTO

Franz Joseph Haydn
(1732 - 1809)

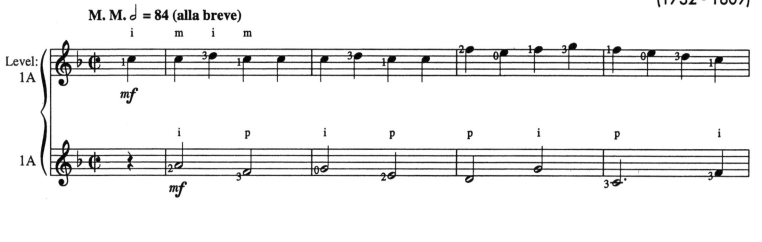

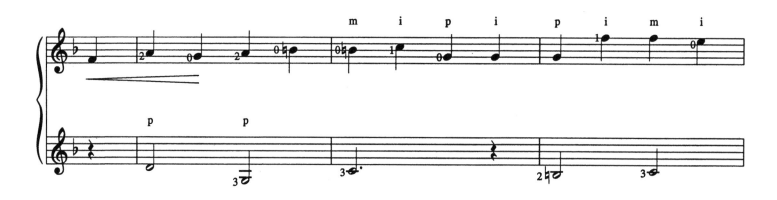

THE EMPEROR WALTZ

Johann Strauss
(1825 - 1899)

AIR

Henry Purcell
(1658 - 1695)

BOURÉE

Johann Sebastian Bach
(1685 - 1750)

THEME
from *FANTASIE IMPROMPTU*

Frederic Chopin
(1810 - 1849)

EL VITO

Traditional Spanish

ADAGIO

Ferdinand Carulli
(1770 - 1841)

CHORALE

Johann Sebastian Bach
(1685 - 1750)

MINUET

Franz Joseph Haydn
(1732 - 1809)

RONDINO

Jean Philippe-Rameau
(1683 - 1764)

SONATINA

Anton Andre
(1775 - 1842)

MELODY

Robert Schumann
(1810 - 1856)

MISTRESS WINTER'S JUMP

John Dowland
(1562 - 1626)

29

CINQUE-PACE GALLIARD

Anon. 16th c.

SARABANDE

Arcangelo Corelli
(1653 - 1713)

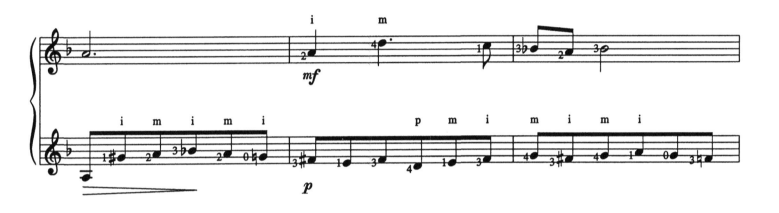

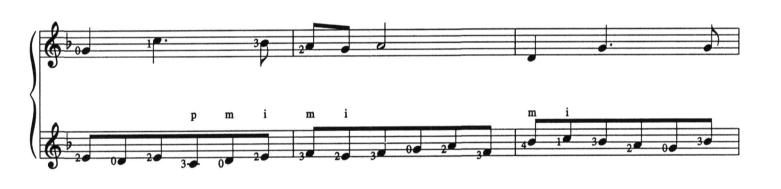

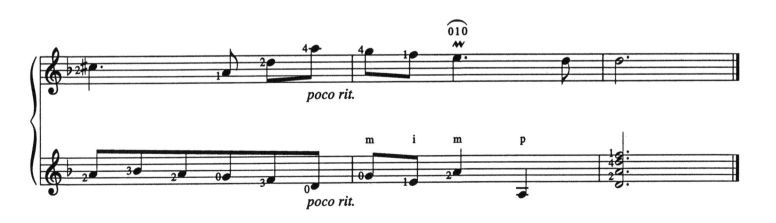

SONATINA

Ferdinand Carulli
(1770 - 1841)

THEME
from *SYMPHONY No. 1*

Johannes Brahms
(1833 - 1897)

GAVOTTE

George Frideric Handel
(1685 - 1759)

MINUET

Johann Sebastian Bach
(1685 - 1750)

LE PETIT RIEN

Francois Couperin
(1668 - 1733)

CLEMENT'S SQUIRREL

Anon., 16th c.

MINUET
from *VIENNA SONATINA*

Wolfgang Amadeus Mozart
(1756 - 1791)

poco a poco crescendo

"AYLESFORD" AIR

George Frideric Handel
(1685 - 1759)

PAVANE, Op. 50

Gabriel Fauré
(1830 - 1914)

CLASSICAL GUITAR

INSTRUCTIONAL BOOKS & METHODS AVAILABLE FROM HAL LEONARD

CLASSICAL STUDIES FOR PICK-STYLE GUITAR
by William Leavitt
Berklee Press
This Berklee Workshop, featuring over 20 solos and duets by Bach, Carcassi, Paganini, Sor and other renowned composers, is designed to acquaint intermediate to advanced pick-style guitarists with some of the excellent classical music that is adaptable to pick-style guitar. With study and practice, this workshop will increase a player's knowledge and proficiency on this formidable instrument.
50449440...$14.99

ÉTUDES SIMPLES FOR GUITAR
by Leo Brouwer
Editions Max Eschig
This new, completely revised and updated edition includes critical commentary and performance notes. Each study is accompanied by an introduction that illustrates its principal musical features and technical objectives, complete with suggestions and preparatory exercises.
50565810 Book/CD Pack.......................$26.99

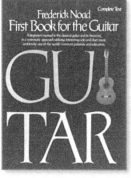

FIRST BOOK FOR THE GUITAR
by Frederick Noad
G. Schirmer, Inc.
A beginner's manual to the classical guitar. Uses a systematic approach using the interesting solo and duet music written by Noad, one of the world's foremost guitar educators. No musical knowledge is necessary. Student can progress by simple stages. Many of the exercises are designed for a teacher to play with the students. Will increase student's enthusiasm, therefore increasing the desire to take lessons.
50334370 Part 1.......................................$12.99
50334520 Part 2.......................................$18.99
50335160 Part 3.......................................$16.99
50336760 Complete Edition....................$32.99

HAL LEONARD CLASSICAL GUITAR METHOD
by Paul Henry
This comprehensive and easy-to-use beginner's guide uses the music of the master composers to teach you the basics of the classical style and technique. Includes pieces by Beethoven, Bach, Mozart, Schumann, Giuliani, Carcassi, Bathioli, Aguado, Tarrega, Purcell, and more. Includes all the basics plus info on PIMA technique, two- and three-part music, time signatures, key signatures, articulation, free stroke, rest stroke, composers, and much more.
00697376 Book/Online Audio (no tab).................$16.99
00142652 Book/Online Audio (with tab) $17.99

A MODERN APPROACH TO CLASSICAL GUITAR
by Charles Duncan
This multi-volume method was developed to allow students to study the art of classical guitar within a new, more contemporary framework. For private, class or self-instruction.
00695114 Book 1 – Book Only..............................$8.99
00695113 Book 1 – Book/Online Audio................$12.99
00699204 Book 1 – Repertoire Book Only............$11.99
00699205 Book 1 – Repertoire Book/Online Audio .$16.99
00695116 Book 2 – Book Only..............................$8.99
00695115 Book 2 – Book/Online Audio................$12.99
00699208 Book 2 – Repertoire...............................$12.99
00699202 Book 3 – Book Only..............................$9.99
00695117 Book 3 – Book/Online Audio................$14.99
00695119 Composite Book/CD Pack....................$32.99

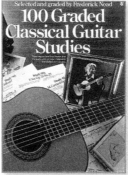

100 GRADED CLASSICAL GUITAR STUDIES
Selected and Graded by Frederick Noad
Frederick Noad has selected 100 studies from the works of three outstanding composers of the classical period: Sor, Giuliani, and Carcassi. All these studies are invaluable for developing both right hand and left hand skills. Students and teachers will find this book invaluable for making technical progress. In addition, they will build a repertoire of some of the most melodious music ever written for the guitar.
14023154..$29.99

CHRISTOPHER PARKENING GUITAR METHOD
THE ART & TECHNIQUE OF THE CLASSICAL GUITAR
Guitarists will learn basic classical technique by playing over 50 beautiful classical pieces, 26 exercises and 14 duets, and through numerous photos and illustrations. The method covers: rudiments of classical technique, note reading and music theory, selection and care of guitars, strategies for effective practicing, and much more!
00696023 Book 1/Online Audio $22.99
00695228 Book 1 (No Audio) $17.99
00696024 Book 2/Online Audio $22.99
00695229 Book 2 (No Audio) $17.99

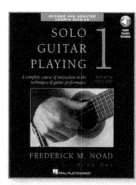

SOLO GUITAR PLAYING
by Frederick M. Noad
Solo Guitar Playing can teach even the person with no previous musical training how to progress from simple single-line melodies to mastery of the guitar as a solo instrument. Fully illustrated with diagrams, photographs, and over 200 musical exercises and repertoire selections, these books offer instruction in every phase of classical guitar playing.
14023147 Book 1/Online Audio $34.99
14023153 Book 1 (Book Only) $24.99
14023151 Book 2 (Book Only) $19.99

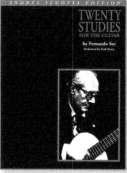

TWENTY STUDIES FOR THE GUITAR
ANDRÉS SEGOVIA EDITION
by Fernando Sor
Performed by Paul Henry
20 studies for the classical guitar written by Beethoven's contemporary, Fernando Sor, revised, edited and fingered by the great classical guitarist Andres Segovia. These essential repertoire pieces continue to be used by teachers and students to build solid classical technique. Features 50-minute demonstration audio.
00695012 Book/Online Audio $22.99
00006363 Book Only...$9.99